DISCOVERING YOUR INDIVIDUAL WORTH

Helping Teens Find More Personal Peace

ANDREW T. WRIGHT

Published by KHARIS PUBLISHING, imprint of KHARIS MEDIA LLC.

Copyright © 2021 Andrew T. Wright

ISBN-13: 978-1-63746-065-8

ISBN-10: 1-63746-065-1

Library of Congress Control Number: 2021937716

All Scripture quotations, unless otherwise indicated, are taken from The King James Version®. Used by permission. All rights reserved worldwide.

All KHARIS PUBLISHING products are available at special quantity discounts for bulk purchase for sales promotions, premiums, fund-raising, and educational needs. For details, contact:

Kharis Media LLC
Tel: 1-479-599-8657
support@kharispublishing.com
www.kharispublishing.com

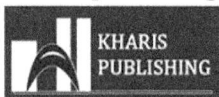

CONTENTS

SECTION ONE: Our Purpose Defined

1   An Introduction   1

2   Combating the Curse of Comparison   7

3   The Key to Achieving Peaceful Joy—Your Infinite, Individual Worth   13

4   How will this Discovery Help?   23

5   Some Disclaimers   33

SECTION TWO: Principles for Discovering Your Infinite Individual Worth

6   Step One to Discovering Your Self-Worth — Seek to Serve   37

7   Serving in Small, Simple, and Continuous Ways   43

8   A Simple Service Act—Kindness   49

9   Step Two to Discovery—Choose a Challenge   57

10   Step Three to Discovery—Give Gratitude   67

11   Step Four to Discovery—Discover Deity   79

12   Conclusion—Escaping the Curse of Comparison   97

Cited Works / Reference   101

SECTION ONE

OUR PURPOSE DEFINED

CHAPTER ONE

AN INTRODUCTION

*"No one is without troubles, without personal
hardships and genuine challenges.
Nobody, not even the purest heart, escapes life
without suffering battle scars."*—Richelle E. Goodrich

Junior High and High School

I hated junior high. Really hated it. If I could somehow edit my life, like people edit films or essays, I would definitely edit out sixth, seventh, and eighth grade. Try to picture the most awkward middle schooler in the history of existence and you'll have a pretty good idea of what I was like. First off, I did not possess even an iota of social skill, neither did I belong to any clique/group; I wasn't a jock or a stoner or a hick or a nerd. So, I was deemed a social misfit and a loner. In addition, I could never seem to wear the right clothes (actually my wife tells me I still don't), and I played the violin (I don't know about your school, but in my school, violin playing wasn't really the key to popularity). Add those elements to my large, dark-rimmed glasses and giant buck teeth and it was a pretty awkward combination. Like I said, I hated junior high.

High school, on the other hand, was a totally different story. By that time, I had found my friendship group (actually, *they* found *me*), I was doing well in my classes and in some school extra-curricular activities, and, would you believe it? I had kind of learned how to talk to people (except when I was on a date, then all social skills seemed to magically disappear again). Life in high school was pretty good.

As I look back on those times what is interesting to me is that I had struggles and challenges but also good times and successes in both schools. Although I loved high school, there were still some really challenging moments, while, conversely, there were times when junior high, for all my distaste of it, brought me pure joy (like when I beat my whole P.E. class in "Lightning").

Your Experience

As a high school teacher, I work with teenagers nearly every day—kids who, because of some problems at home or peer relationships or emotional issues, are struggling. They wonder why they have such a dysfunctional family, why they don't have friends, why their body isn't like someone else's, or why nobody understands them. It might surprise you to know that it's not just the students with the more obvious challenges who struggle. Sometimes the most athletic or the most attractive or the most outgoing student is also struggling… a lot. These popular students, too, sometimes feel like nobody understands them and/or that the world is stacked against them. Life can be really challenging for them as well.

This begs the following questions: How do you deal with your own challenges? Are you struggling with an obvious setback, or are your struggles less obvious to your family, teachers, and friends? Are you someone who feels like your challenges are overwhelming or do you feel like they come and go as often as the common cold? Do you feel like you're the only one in your family who is experiencing these struggles? Or perhaps you know that other people have challenges like yours, but those other kids seem to handle their challenges much better than you? Or maybe you think you're somewhere in-between struggling and contentment, depending on how well you did on your test this week or how many people said "hi" to you in the hall. Or maybe your life is, on the whole, pretty good, but occasionally you have a rough stretch that really gets you down.

You Are Not Alone

Whatever situation you are now in, an important purpose of this book is to assure you that you are not alone. You might feel alone, and think that there is no one who understands you or who wants to help, but I want you to know that those thoughts are simply not true.

There are two important indicators that you are not alone. First, there are other people all around you, every day, who also have problems and challenges. These people might hide their problems better than you, they might appear like they are cruising through life without any care in the world, but they are not. They are having to battle just like you. Because of this, you certainly don't need to feel ashamed or embarrassed if you are struggling. And you should never feel like you have to hide your struggles or your challenges from those who are close to you (although certainly you don't need to broadcast them to everyone either). As one of my favorite public speakers, Jeffrey R. Holland, once said, "The trials of life can be very deep and we are not shallow people if we struggle with them."[1] It's okay to struggle. We all do.

Help for the Difficult Journey

The second indicator that you are not alone is the fact that there are also people all around you who would love to help you, no matter what situation you are in. Now I know from my own junior high school days that these people might sometimes seem hard to find, but they exist, I promise. My writing this book is, in its own way, my attempt to be one of those people. Of course, I don't have all the answers, but I am one of the many who are ready to help out in whatever way we can. I do this—try to help you in a small way—because I remember, just as clear as day, that sometimes being a teenager is really hard.

The Challenges of Teenage-hood

I have to tell you, I've spent many hours trying to understand why being a teenager is so hard. I am sure there are a lot of different answers, but my own personal conclusion is that being a teenager is especially difficult because, in contrast to old people like me who are fairly set in our ways, so much of your world is constantly changing: your body, your emotions, your friends, everything. You might have a friend today who, by this time tomorrow, won't even talk to you anymore and you have no idea why. Or your emotions may suddenly go haywire, and you can't even give yourself, let alone your friends, a good reason as to why you suddenly hate the whole world, when just the day before everything seemed wonderful. And, to complicate things even more, all these changes and challenges come at a time when you're still trying to discover who you are and where your place is in the world.

Because of all these challenges, I would like to express my most sincere solicitude for all the awkwardness / drama / unpredictability/anxiety of teenage-hood that you have had to endure. I know it isn't easy and I know that sometimes it might seem like this part of your life will never wrap up, but I want to assure you that there is a lot of peace and happiness to be discovered *if* you learn to look in the right place.

My Goal

My hope in writing this book is to give you the tools so that when your life's journey hits a bump in the road (it's sometimes more like a mountain in the road) you will still be able to have a feeling which I like to call "peaceful joy." Whether your challenge is a rough week (like I had in high school when I discovered the girl of my dreams didn't know I existed), or a rough year… or three (like basically my whole junior high experience), I'm hoping that some of the principles you learn in these chapters will help. I'm hoping you will be better equipped to feel peaceful joy even during the numerous challenges which might be constantly bombarding you.

In my writing, I am not going to cite and/or analyze all the numerous sociological studies which have been done on the topic of self-esteem or self-confidence (although personally I find some of those studies pretty interesting and useful). Rather, I feel like it will be most helpful to you if I simply relate what I've learned through my experience as a high school teacher and then encourage you to put these lessons into action. (And I can't emphasize enough that the power of these principles is not in the words, but in the action.)

One final note as we begin: As you read, I would like you to think of this book as something of a workbook. As I outline some steps to help you, I will also include a few assignments to accompany the discussion points. But don't worry, the assignments won't be hard and even more importantly, there won't be any grades attached.

Assignment:

- After reading the first chapter, how do you feel about your own situation and your own challenges? Do you feel like you regularly feel at peace or are you overwhelmed by your trials?

CHAPTER TWO

COMBATING THE CURSE OF COMPARISON

"Comparison is the thief to joy." —Theodore Roosevelt

Before we go any further, I have a pretty important confession to make: I do not have all the answers (shocking, I know). There are lots of problems and challenges in life for which I don't have any adequate explanation or advice. Sorry, I really wish I did, but I'm not nearly that smart. However, as I've thought about the things that young people struggle with, and listened to the hundreds of stories my students tell me about their lives, I've determined that so many teenage struggles are tied to what I like to call "The Curse of Comparison." We live in a culture which is totally obsessed with comparing and competing. So many voices are shouting at us that "you need to be smarter, faster, stronger, or prettier." They are constantly saying, "It really is important who you hang out with and how many people like you and how many sports teams you play on."

And, because of social media, I'm fairly certain your challenges with the curse of comparison might be even more intense than past generations—who can get the most likes? Who has the cutest pictures? Who has the cleverest tweets? Of course, not all your teenage struggles will come from these comparisons, but many will. These specific struggles, those which have to do with our society's obsession with comparing ourselves to each other, are the specific struggles I would like to address in this book. Whether these comparisons are based on looks, or athletic ability, or smarts, or shoe size, or whatever, "these things ought not so to be"[2] These constant comparisons and competitions destroy peaceful joy and often leave in its place feelings of anxiety, stress, frustration, and depression.

A Natural Reaction

During my teenage years, I was always comparing myself to the people around me in junior high, and I never felt like I measured up. That's one of the major reasons why junior high was such a miserable experience.

These observations about the curse of comparison have led me to ask the question, "Why?" Why do we so often compare if these comparisons so frequently create such negative results? Why do our interactions so often end up turning into some sort of competition? It certainly doesn't have to be this way. Why didn't I then, and why don't teenagers now, more naturally and more often support and admire each other, instead of comparing and coveting.

I believe one reason is because the competitive drive might simply be a part of our nature as humans. For some people (which would definitely include myself), comparing and competing seems to be a natural reaction. For example, let me tell you a story from last year when my kids and I were at a park playing. As we were getting ready to leave, they both asked me to get them some leaves off a tree so they could look at them on our drive home (apparently leaves are very fascinating to 6- and 4-year-olds). Interestingly, the first thing they did after I gave each of them a leaf, was to start comparing with each other. They wanted to see who had the "cooler" leaf. To me, it seemed like it was just a natural reaction, something they did without much thought. In any case, I can assure you that my wife and I have not spent one second teaching them that having a cool leaf is the key to childhood happiness.

This tendency to compare seems similar to the natural desire some of us have to stop running the second we start to feel a little tired or our natural desire to walk out of math class the second we encounter a problem that is too hard (which is basically every problem, if you are like me and have zero math skills). I am not a psychologist or a sociologist, but it seems to me that the temptation to compare ourselves with others is an element of many of our natures, similar to selfishness or generosity.

Contemporary Culture

However, another part of the answer to this question of "Why?" has to be that comparisons, especially in the form of competition, have become a deeply imbedded element of teenage culture. As I'm sure you know, so much of a teenager's life revolves around—and is tied to—comparison: grades, social media posts, sports, dating, fashion, and plenty of other things. Our culture has adopted a comparative approach and it affects nearly everything we do. We are constantly told we need to do more building. We need to build a stronger resumé; we need to build our self-worth, build a better GPA, and build more friendships.

Society has convinced us that if we have more of something, life will be better. As Houston Kraft, in his book *Deep Kindness,* writes, "For many of us, we are just quietly programmed by culture to believe that we simply aren't *enough.* We need better grades; we need to be about three inches taller. Your chest isn't burly enough and your stomach isn't flat enough. Your job doesn't make enough money, your house isn't fancy enough, and your photos don't get enough likes. You're not smart enough, beautiful enough, fast enough, or successful enough."[3]

A House Built on Sand

And, I should note that this principle applies to both the negative *and* positive things that people might think or say about you. When somebody compliments you, it is really easy to internalize that message as well and to start thinking that you are somehow "better" than every other person around you. But this also is not good. Thinking too much of yourself can be just as dangerous as not thinking enough of yourself.

Have you ever heard the parable of the foolish man who built his house upon the sand?[4] That little story is what I think of when I see people put too much importance on the praise they receive from other people. It is certainly nice to be praised and to be liked. But be careful; if you start depending on the praise and compliments of others, if your perception of who you are becomes tied to others' thoughts about you, you're building your house on sand. At some point, those positive comments will be gone (and they might even turn negative), the rain will come, and your house will be washed right away. I've seen this happen too many times to count and believe me, it is a painful thing to observe.

Don't Believe the Noise

Now I totally get that it can be really hard to not let what other people say or write or post about you influence what you think about yourself. I mean, let's be honest, when you hear somebody say something really great about you (especially from someone you have a huge crush on) you naturally feel good. And, when you hear or read something negative about yourself, you naturally feel not so good.

So, a little clarification and explanation might be helpful. I'm not saying there's anything wrong with some person's unkind (or kind) comments *affecting* you. I am certainly not trying to turn you into some unfeeling, bionic creature. Being affected by others is natural; it's just part of who we are as humans. If, for example, your coach yells at you every time you breathe, making you feel like the worst player on the planet, it will not be surprising if that makes you so mad you want to punch that coach in the face; or if it makes you so unbearably sad that you just want to lay in bed and cry...for a month. Or, on the flip side, if your favorite teacher pays you a compliment, there's certainly no problem being on top of the world for a day or two. Having feelings and emotions just means you're human (although, obviously, I don't think too many coaches should actually be punched in the face).

The problem isn't really in letting the actions and opinions of others affect you, the problem and danger come when you start to *believe* those people. It's okay to feel sad or hurt when you know that someone thinks you're not pretty or handsome enough. What's not okay is for you to start believing that what that person says is true; to start believing that being yourself is somehow not enough. It's

11

all right for someone to affect you, it's not all right for someone to convince you. A major purpose of this book is making sure that doesn't happen.

Whatever the reason for your constantly comparing yourself to others—whether it's from the culture that surrounds you (nurture) or just part of your nature, (or perhaps a combination of both)—,it is time to escape the cultural curse of comparison and create a life where you can more easily access peaceful joy. People fight their desire to stop running because they don't want to get out of shape (or they want to get in shape), high school students fight their desire to walk out of math class because they don't want an "F." You and I should try to more consistently battle our desire to compare because our comparing and competing will, either sooner or later, leave us feeling like "we are never enough."

Assignment:

- In what aspects of your life do you compare yourself to others the most? And what do you think is the reason this happens?

CHAPTER THREE

THE KEY TO ACHIEVING PEACEFUL JOY—YOUR INFINITE, INDIVIDUAL WORTH

One human life is worth more than all the treasures of the earth. —Seth Adam Smith

Infinite, Individual Worth

All of this leads us to the big question: How do I plan on helping you conquer this temptation to constantly compare, compete, and covet so that you can experience more peaceful joy? How can I help you break free from this culture which thrives on the curse of comparison and instead get you to the point where you realize that what other people think simply doesn't matter?

Obviously, it would be fantastic if I could simply wave a magic wand and get rid of our culture's obsession with comparison. But I don't think that's possible (I'm a muggle, after all). So, having accepted that fact, instead of trying to change society, I would like to assist you in changing how you perceive society. This I know is possible.

Maybe you've had an experience like this one: Once in high school, I was having a really terrible day. Something or someone had done something to upset me and my anger was building (although I don't remember exactly what it was). Knowing that I needed to somehow deal with my anger that night, I went over to my friend's—Stephen's—house and had a great late-night discussion/venting session.[5] Of course, just like I knew would happen, after that chat, I felt so much better. However, after a couple of weeks, much to my dismay, I realized that my nice chat had indeed made me feel better for that night and the next week, but, in the long run, it hadn't done much to actually solve the problem.

What I've learned over time from experiences like this, and others, is that there are lots of temporary treatments for our curse of comparison challenges. In addition to a nice chat with a friend, you could also listen to a really good song, spend some time alone or, best of all, eat a gallon of really good ice cream. These things would undoubtedly help you cope with your struggles in the short term, and they really can be useful if you need a quick pick-me-up. But the drawback is that their effects are usually ephemeral. Their influence will likely wear off, and your challenges will still be there, and long-lasting peaceful joy will have eluded you.

The way I see it, these temporary treatments can be like trying to treat a broken arm with some pain killer. I'm no doctor but I'm pretty sure that simply taking some strong pain killer, although very useful, won't really solve the problem of the broken arm. Without treatment for the actual break, the medicine won't remedy the problem and might even make things worse if there isn't proper treatment. Instead, something else is needed to make sure the arm heals properly. It needs to be set in a cast and regularly examined, etc. It is the same with the challenges which come from the curse of comparison. Lots of things we do to help us cope might make us feel better in the short term, but they probably don't actually provide a long-term fix.

What I want to help you discover is a long-term solution, a permanent fix to help the inner you escape the curse of comparison. *This permanent fix entails discovering your infinite, individual worth.* I believe this discovery is vital if you want to experience genuine peace and joy throughout your life. Nothing, and I mean nothing, will help you conquer the curse of comparison and experience peaceful joy more than knowing that you have infinite worth.

What Does Infinite, Individual Worth Mean?

Have you ever seen the movie *The Incredibles*? (I hope the answer is yes.) I really love that show. However, I have to confess that there is one part of the movie I do have a little problem with. If you're a Pixar connoisseur you might remember the part where Dash and his mom (Helen Parr, a.k.a. Elastigirl) are driving home from school after Dash gets in trouble for putting a tack on his teacher's chair (By the way, I have had students put tacks on my chair before. Not fun.) They are talking about how to best use their superpowers when their discussion starts to get a little heated. As they go back and forth, Helen says, "Everyone's special, Dash." To which Dash responds, "Which is just another way of saying no one is."

Now no offense to Dash (I'm sure he's a very intelligent little boy), but I'm here to tell you that Dashiell Robert Parr is wrong. Every person truly *is* special, no matter who they are, what they can do, or where they are from.

To emphasize my point, let me quote from another movie which isn't as well known as *The Incredibles*, but is just as

15

good (that is, if you like movies totally in German that have a lot of talking and no action). The movie is called *Sophie Scholl;* it's about a brother and sister in Germany who oppose Hitler. Their opposition is mainly accomplished by publishing and distributing pamphlets outlining all the lies Hitler is telling his people. At the beginning of the movie, the Scholls are passing out their pamphlets at a university and are caught. After their capture, they are interrogated by a detective named Herr Mohr. During the interrogation, Sophie, in response to a statement from the detective, says with a lot of emotion, "Every life is precious." As opposed to Dash's statement, this one from Sophie Scholl is something I totally agree with: every life truly is precious, everyone has worth, including you.

And how special are you? How precious are you? Infinitely. In case you never go to your math class (which is totally understandable), in math, infinite refers to an amount that is greater than any regular number. In my view, this is a perfectly analogous to your worth. Whether you believe it or not, no matter who you are or where you are, you are very precious, worth more than any regular number.

Is Your Eye More Important than Your Ear?

In the New Testament, the Apostle Paul, in a letter written to people in a place called Corinth, had some very insightful comments about the worth of individuals.[6] I have included those verses here. However, since the verses are written in 1600s English which is not always understandable, I've added my 21st century translation in italics.

Paul wrote,

"For the body is not one member but many. And the foot shall say, because I am not the hand, I am not of the body and the ear shall say, because I am not the eye I am not of the body.

"If the whole body were an eye, where were the hearing? If the whole were hearing, where were the smelling. If they were all one member, where were the body? And the eye cannot say to the hand, I have no need of thee, nor again the head to the feet, I have no need of you."

And then this, which is my favorite:

"Nay, much more those members of the body which seem to be more feeble are necessary."

And now for my translation:

*"There are so many different types of people. Just because you're not like somebody else, **does not** mean you don't have value or that you are not important.*

Everybody's unique traits are needed. A human body functions precisely because it has many different parts which have totally different roles. So too does the human race. We need all types and anybody that thinks otherwise is just plain wrong.

If you think you are the most unimportant person around, that you don't have anything to add to society, you have it backwards. You are just as "necessary" and important as anybody else."

I love that little lesson from Paul. No matter who you are, or what role you play in this big world, you are important. You have infinite worth.

Self-Worth Is Not Self-Confidence

Here I would like to make an important clarification. I believe it is crucial to understand that when I refer to your individual worth, I am referring to something that cannot be changed, altered, or developed. As you've probably noticed, sometimes our culture gets pretty obsessed with developing and building self-esteem, self-respect, and self-confidence. There are lots and lots of books and articles about these subjects. But when I talk about infinite, individual self-worth, I am *not* talking about self-respect, self-confidence, or self-esteem (although these things are very important). Confidence, respect, and esteem can be, and usually are, constantly changing, but your value, your worth does not and cannot change, no matter what.

Now just so you're aware, there are some very well-meaning people in this world who will try very hard to persuade you to believe otherwise. They will try to convince you that your worth and your self-confidence/self-esteem are the same or, at a minimum, closely tied together. Those people will argue that right now you're maybe worth a penny, but if you do this and that, you could be worth a million dollars.[7] No doubt the people who hold this view are well-meaning individuals, but I would like to very respectfully disagree with them.

Don't get me wrong, as I mentioned earlier, you *can* (and should) develop your self-esteem, your self-respect, and your self-confidence. These are very important in realizing your potential as an individual, and in being successful in many other endeavors. Self-confidence is often an important determining factor in your performance on a test, in an interview, or in a game. If your dream is to be the star of the basketball team or a concert pianist, you will need a healthy dose of self-confidence to achieve that goal.

But neither potential nor confidence are equal to worth. Individual worth is different. Your *perception* of your worth might change, and other people's perception of your worth might change. But your worth itself, the value of you, does not change.

I had a student who was awesome at test taking. Honestly, his scores were unbelievable. I'm sure his confidence was always sky high whenever test day came around. On the other hand, I have students each year who would rather do just about anything else in this world than take any sort of test. I just say the word "test" and they look like they might pass out (or start a mutiny). However, there is nobody on this planet who could convince me that my test-hating students are somehow worth less than my test-loving student, although their confidence levels (and consequently test scores) are often very different.

In high school, I had a lot of confidence when I was on the soccer field or in a choir concert, but much less confidence in my chemistry class (science and I do not get along). But even though my confidence was high playing soccer, after a particularly poor game, my confidence might descend lower than the Dead Sea for a day or two. Likewise, on those extremely rare occasions when I understood Ms. Villarta's chemistry lesson, my confidence in my chemistry skills might rise ever so slightly. My self-confidence was always changing, depending on the circumstances of that day. The same could be said of my self-esteem. If somebody had charted my self-esteem level in high school, the chart would have resembled something like the world's craziest roller-coaster, constantly going up and down.

So yes, confidence and self-esteem might be constantly changing, but it's important to understand your worth is not.

Three $100 Bills

Imagine that I have several $100 bills (which, when you consider the fact that I'm a schoolteacher, will require quite the imagination) and I give one to each of my three children. One of my kids keeps the bill in their wallet, carries it with them everywhere, and is eager to show it to all their friends. Another one of my kids takes the bill and puts it in a picture frame because it is very special to them. They have no intention of spending it; they just enjoy staring at it and knowing that they own it. Finally, another child promptly loses the money I give them somewhere in their room, and are not sure where it is exactly.

Several weeks later, this child who lost the money decides they would really like to buy themselves a new unicycle. With their mind made up, they rip their room apart looking for the money. Finally, after hours of searching and a fair amount of frustration, they finally find the bill under their bed, crumpled up, with a little tear and some unknown liquid on it.

How much is that bill worth compared to his siblings'? Well, you know the answer to that question (at least hopefully you do). All three bills are worth exactly the same, no matter what physical state they are in. That same principle applies to us as individuals. We are all worth the same, no matter our physical state, no matter how many skills and abilities we have or don't have. The only difference is that each of us is worth much more than $100.

Assignment:

- How would you rate your own perception of your individual worth right now? In your honest opinion, how much do you think you're worth compared to your friends and family?

CHAPTER FOUR

HOW WILL THIS DISCOVERY HELP?

"One day he met a Wemmick [who] . . . had no dots or stars. It wasn't that people didn't try to give her stickers; it's just that the stickers didn't stick."
—Max Lucado

The aim of this book is not to develop or increase your worth, it is already there, and it is already infinite. Rather, I hope to help you discover this worth. But not only do I want you to discover that your worth is infinite, I also want you to discover that the knowledge of your worth can be life-changing. It will fill your life with peaceful joy like no other discovery. It will be more powerful than a late-night chat with your best friend. It will be more powerful than the most recent motivational TED talk. It will change your life and you will find a whole new, and much better, perspective.

How Does this Help?

How will discovering your infinite, individual worth help you escape our culture's curse of comparison and be filled with peaceful joy? How can this discovery be so important and so powerful?

Well, I believe the answer lies in the fact that when you truly understand that your individual worth is infinite, that every life, including your own, is in fact precious, you will begin to understand that so many of your problems and challenges and trials are on the outside of you. They are relentlessly trying to attack you, to overwhelm you, but, this is the key: they are not you. You will begin to understand that much of what you have been internalizing your whole life actually has nothing to do with who you really are.

Punchinello and the Wemmicks

I love the book *You are Special* by Max Lucado. It explains this principle much better than I—and any other book I've read—ever could. If you haven't read it, please try and read it. In the story, the characters, who are called Wemmicks, are always trying to label one another as either good or bad. They do this by putting stickers on each other (a gold star for good things, a gray dot for the bad). One day, an awkward little Wemmick named Punchinello (he reminds me of myself in junior high) meets another Wemmick named Lucia who doesn't have any stars or dots stuck to her. Punchinello finds this fascinating; he is sure every Wemmick has at least some stickers on them. With his curiosity peaked, the rest of the book details Punchinellos quest to figure out why there are no stickers on Lucia.

By the end of the book, he has discovered some very important lessons and is beginning to understand the concept of individual worth. One important message from the story is that, just like Lucia, we also should learn how to not let any of the stickers' stick—the good or bad ones. Our goal should be to understand that what other people think, whether negative or positive, isn't as important as we sometimes believe it is.

This message is illustrated well towards the end of the book where we read:

> "Eli stooped down and picked [Punchinello] up and set him on the bench. 'Hmm,' the maker spoke thoughtfully as he looked at the gray dots. 'Looks like you've been given some bad marks.'
>
> 'I didn't mean to, Eli. I really tried hard.'
>
> 'Oh, you don't have to defend yourself to me, child. I don't care what the other Wemmicks think.'
>
> 'You don't?'
>
> 'No, and you shouldn't either. Who are they to give stars or dots? They're Wemmicks just like you. What they think doesn't matter, Punchinello.'"[8]

I agree with Eli. What people think doesn't matter. Your worth is not determined by anyone or anything. It is already infinite, even if some people (including yourself) keep trying to give you gray dots or gold stars.

Internalizing Comparisons

Of course, that is easier said than believed right. For example, you might be in school right now and your classes might be really hard and you might be really struggling. And because of this, you might have been given the label of unsmart (by yourself or by your classmates or by your teacher). Or maybe your skin color or your nationality or your religion isn't the same as those around you. Or maybe all your friends have boyfriends (or girlfriends), yet you can't seem to find a date no matter how nice you try to do your hair or how much cologne you put on.

In these situations, and many others, you and a whole lot of other people can be pretty easily persuaded that the problem is actually us, that our value isn't as high as the value of the smart people or the pretty people or the strong people.

As we become consumed by this curse of comparison, we begin to evaluate our worth through the lens of these constant comparisons and critiques. We begin to think that because we aren't as cool as the person sitting next to us in history class, we aren't worth as much as they are. Or because we don't have as many friends as that popular kid, we're not worth as much as they are. Or perhaps we might think, "Maybe the really talented person has worth, but not me; I come from a home where my parents are drug addicts." Or "I'm not worth much, I'm constantly getting in trouble and none of my teachers can stand having me in class." Or "I'm a failure. Everything I touch is ruined. Surely I'm not worth as much as Taylor Swift or LeBron James or Oprah."

As Houston Kraft, whom I quoted earlier, writes, "External commentary [becomes] internal criticism. [This criticism] is a lie that… came from the outside and, now that we've repeated it for so long, we only hear in our own voice. This subtle shift from 'You' to 'I' is among the most damaging transitions we could experience. 'You'll never be as good as them' becomes 'I'll never be any good.' 'You're useless. You're a burden' becomes 'I deserve to be alone.' 'You need to do better. You're a disappointment' becomes 'I'm not enough.'"[9]

I know it's hard to break out from this mindset, but I'm

here to tell you that if you are thinking any of these "not enough" thoughts, you are wrong. All these ideas, all these negative thoughts that sometimes come from you and sometimes come from others, they are all based on comparison and competition. These misperceptions are coming from the environment, trying to destroy your peaceful joy (and too often they are successful).

Thankfully, you now have this long-term solution at our fingertips to help you escape these lies (because that is exactly what all these comparisons are). As you begin to understand that no matter what is happening around you, you have infinite, individual worth, you will become more and more protected from these comparisons. This doesn't mean that some challenges won't knock you down or cause you pain, but you will be able to recover from these attacks in a way that you never would have thought possible. You will be able to experience a powerful inner peace.

Tight like unto a Dish

Let me tell you just one more story illustrating this principle; it's actually sort of a metaphor. In a collection of writings from an ancient civilization,[10] there's a story about a group of people who crossed an ocean in ships which they said were "tight like unto a dish." Now I realize that "tight like unto a dish" is kind of a weird phrase and you are right now probably wondering, "Wait a second, what does that even mean?"

Well, I confess I'm not sure I totally understand, but it seems likely that in those days (thousands of years ago), there were probably a lot of different items they might have been forced to use for eating which wouldn't have been very useful in holding food or liquid (try eating or drinking from a leaf for example). Apparently, what they called dishes were really great at being "tight" and not letting anything spill. So, when the author wrote that his ships were "tight like unto a dish," he was referring to the idea that because the ships were sealed, nothing was able to hurt them or stop them or damage them. Not anything. While the waves were raging all around them, inside the ship there was peace.

As it says in the writings, "[The ships] were tossed upon the waves of the sea before the wind. And... they were many times buried in the depths of the sea because of the mountain waves... and also the great and terrible tempests. And...when they were buried in the deep, there was no water that could hurt them, their vessels being tight like unto a dish."[11]

My goal is to help you understand that discovering your infinite, individual worth will create a protection for you which will be "tight like unto a dish." Then, as you cross your own ocean of storms and troubles, (which will come just as surely as you will be bored out of your mind in your next history class), you will not be "buried in the deep." Instead, you will have peaceful joy.

Still Skeptical

Perhaps you are thinking, "This all sounds good, but let's be serious, discovering my worth won't do anything to change my body type or make me more attractive." Or maybe you are thinking, "Knowing I have value might be nice, I suppose, but it won't help me find friends, or help with my social skills." And I will certainly acknowledge that it is true that understanding your individual worth probably won't solve or take away your immediate problems. For example, if you're being bullied at school, this most likely won't stop the bullies from tripping you in the hall or posting terrible things on social media about people like you. And if you have a really hard time talking to people or fitting it, this knowledge might not help you suddenly develop more effective social skills.

So, you might still be thinking that if you just had a really sweet car (or any car at all) then life would be so much better. Maybe if you were just really good at basketball or baseball or football you wouldn't have the insecurities that you now have. Or if you had a different body type, people would pay more attention to you. Well, perhaps it is true that if you had your wish, some things in life might be easier, but other issues and problems would certainly take their place.

It is true that at some points in your life you will have more serious challenges and trials than at other points, but part of being a human is accepting that you will nearly always have some sort of struggle in your life. I remember when I was single, I was convinced that once I found the girl of my dreams, all my troubles would just melt away, and I would live happily ever after. Fortunately, I did eventually find the girl of my dreams. Unfortunately, my troubles didn't melt away; they just changed into other troubles.

It is for this reason that the purpose of this book is not necessarily to take away your problems; you will always have some sort of challenge and there is so much about your life that I can't really help you with. I can't help you with your friends or your looks or your talents or your grades or any of that stuff, at least not directly (although I do know a pretty great math tutor). But what I'm trying to help you see is that these things are only as important as you make them to be. No matter what challenge you have, always try to pay more attention to the value that is on the inside, and not what is on the outside. After you've discovered your individual worth, use that new-found discovery to feel peaceful joy. This is our purpose.

A Leap of Faith

There is a chance that you've read all of this and you are still skeptical. You might still be convinced that the only way for you to feel better about yourself or for you to overcome your challenges is to be different than you are now; a totally different body, a different brain, or a different life. If you are thinking these things, I'm just going to have to ask you to take this leap of faith and just give the principles I outline in the following chapters a try. Hopefully, as you take this leap, by the end of this book I can convince you that discovering your infinite, individual worth will be a more effective protection for your soul than anything else.

So, whether your struggles are seemingly small or potentially life-threatening, long term or short term, try these principles that I am about to explain to you. See what happens. I promise your life will become filled with more peaceful joy.

Assignment:

- Read *You Are Special* by Max Lucado. What did you learn about individual worth?

CHAPTER FIVE

SOME DISCLAIMERS

"What we obtain too cheap, we esteem too lightly."
—Thomas Paine

Not Easy

I think this is a good time to clarify that what I'm recommending for you is not going to be very easy. After all, as I'm sure you've already discovered, nearly everything worth doing takes effort and time to accomplish. As Kara in one of my favorite TV shows *Supergirl* says, "[This] won't be easy. Nothing worthwhile ever is."

Think of the story of *The Three Little Pigs* (which I used to read regularly with my kids). Remember the two pigs who chose to build their houses out of straw and sticks? Have you ever wondered why they chose those building materials in the first place? I know I have, and I think those two foolish pigs chose sticks and straw because of how quick and easy it was to build a house out of those resources. But in the end, I'm pretty sure the third pig was happy he took the time and extra effort to build his house of bricks, since he's the one that didn't get eaten by the wolf (In my opinion, not getting eaten is always a good thing).

Of course, it is easy for me to make this claim, to sit in my comfortable chair here at my desk and lecture you about how you should be doing all these things that will help you in your life. However, it is much harder for you to come to your own knowledge of this principle. My saying your worth is infinite and unchanging, that this knowledge will help shield you from the curse of comparison, is easy. My attempt to get you to understand and believe this idea is a bit more challenging.

You Will Still Have Struggles

Another thing I think I should warn you about is that, even if you follow everything I suggest, it is important to remember that life's problems will never just go away. I have no doubt that there will always be jerks and bullies. No matter how much you and I wish it were otherwise, those guys will always be around. Not only that, but most of the other problems you have also aren't going away anytime soon. No matter your circumstance, there will always be problems and struggles.

As I mentioned in the last chapter, the purpose then is not to necessarily get rid of your problems, but to help you put them in proper perspective.

A Process, Not an Event

One more thought regarding this task of discovering your worth. It will be helpful if you think of this as a process, not an event. Think of mining gold. Although the first discovery of gold is really exciting, personally I think it would be pretty foolish to say, "Well, I found a little bit of gold, now I'm going home." No, you would keep working to find more (at least I would). Discovering your individual worth is the same. It doesn't come all at once; it will come slowly, over time. That first insight into your worth will be exciting and important, but there will be more. So, be patient and ready to keep searching and discovering.

SECTION TWO

PRINCIPLES FOR DISCOVERING YOUR INFINITE, INDIVIDUAL WORTH

What follows are some key principles regarding how to discover your worth as an individual.

CHAPTER SIX

STEP ONE TO DISCOVERING YOUR SELF WORTH— SEEK TO SERVE

"He who lives only unto himself withers and dies, while he who forgets himself in the service of others grows and blossoms in this life..." —Gordon B. Hinckley

I don't know about you, but when I'm going through a challenge, I typically become pretty obsessed with myself (even more than I usually am). And when I obsess over myself and my problems, I usually experience a little (and sometimes a lot of) self-pity. My basic thought becomes, "Why is my life so hard/challenging/unfair? Why is this happening to me?" I pretty much stop noticing or caring about any of the other people around me and, all I can think about is myself.

If you have also experienced this, you have probably also noticed, as I have, that ironically this focus on self rarely helps. In fact, having experienced my fair share of "wallowing in self-pity" moments, I have discovered an important principle: *you will understand your worth the least when you are focused on yourself.*

With this principle in mind, I am going to invite you to do something totally counter-intuitive. As you begin this journey of discovering your infinite individual worth, I'm actually going to ask you to start by forgetting about yourself and instead start focusing on others (see, I told you it would be counter-intuitive). Why would I ask you to do this? It's because I believe the converse of the previous principle is also true: *you will understand your worth the best when you are focused on others.* Or, as a man named Gordon B. Hinckley once said, "The most effective medicine for the sickness of self-pity is to lose oneself in the service of others."[12]

The religious leader Thomas S. Monson gave us all a pretty good explanation of this principle when he said, "Unless we lose ourselves in service to others, there is little purpose to our own lives. Those who live only for themselves eventually shrivel up and figuratively lose their lives, while those who lose themselves in service to others grow and flourish—and in effect save their lives"[13]

How Service Helps

You might not have ever heard of Christopher Reeve, but when I was growing up, he was really famous. He had played Superman in a really popular film tetralogy (in case you were wondering, "tetralogy" is a fancy word for four related stories) then, tragically, he had become paralyzed from the neck down in a horse-riding accident. A couple of years after his accident, he wrote a book called *Still Me*. In it, he gave the following insight (and remember he was a quadriplegic when he wrote this), "When a catastrophe happens it's easy to feel so sorry for yourself that you can't even see anybody around you…*The way out of that misery or obsession is to focus more on what… other people around you need.* It's very hard to do, and often you have to force yourself, but that is the answer…"[14]

This quote is amazing. It is the perfect explanation for why I chose to put service as the first step to discovering your individual worth. A lot of times, when we are struggling the most, it is because we are focused too much on ourselves and we forget that there are other people in the universe. Or sometimes we might remember there are people around us, but we think that what they are struggling with doesn't compare to what we are struggling with. Serving others helps us combat this distorted view.

As you serve, you will discover that all people, no matter what type of lives they have, whether mega rich or devastatingly poor, whether popular or unpopular, are important and worthy of love and respect. Service will help you see yourself and others as they really are, not as competitors and targets of comparisons, but as wonderful but sometimes struggling individuals who all have equal value and importance. Seeing the value of all is a great way to start developing the comforting feeling of peaceful joy.

Who is My Neighbor?

I'm betting that at some point in your life you've heard the story of the Good Samaritan. If you haven't, today is the day. As you might already know, this story/parable was told by Jesus in response to someone asking Him the question, "Who is my neighbor?" Or, in other words, "Who has value? What type of person is worth serving and helping?" The answer Jesus gave to questioner was very profound.

As you may remember, the parable starts with a man, a Jew, traveling down a road and then getting robbed and beaten up. As he lay there suffering, two people who should have helped him did not, and another person, a Samaritan, who wasn't expected to help him, did.[15] You see, it is important to understand that at that time in history, Samaritans hated, I mean really hated, the Jews. Yet this man, a Samaritan, helped the beaten Jew, even though they were supposed to despise each other. Why did the Samaritan help? Because, as Jesus was trying to teach, "every life is precious." Every single life! Even the person who is most despised or rejected or scorned.

I had a minor but still important experience when I was living in Switzerland as a 20-year-old, which helped me understand that each person has value. While living in Zurich (that's a major city in Switzerland), I often used public transportation to get wherever I needed to go (which was actually quite enjoyable, unless I missed the train, then it was considerably less enjoyable). One day, I got on a tram and started talking to the lady sitting across from me. I don't remember exactly what we talked about, but I do remember I talked to her a little bit about the purpose of life and we had a pretty good conversation about that. Then, after only riding the tram for a couple of stops, she got off. As I watched her walk away, I remember thinking about how crazy it was that literally ten minutes before, I would have seen that person and not thought anything of her. Now, after a learning a little bit about her beliefs, she was suddenly an important person, a person of value.

Let me tell you another story that happened to me recently. I was at work and was asked to take another employee and her daughter home, since their car wasn't working. As we were driving, she told me a little bit about her life. She had seven children, her husband had died recently, and she was struggling to make enough money to support herself and her family. As I dropped her off, I noticed that her house was pretty run down and there were items strewn all over the yard. Honestly, if I had just seen this woman or her house randomly, without getting to know her, I would have probably judged her pretty unfairly (being judgmental is a weakness I have). I would have thought something like: Why didn't this woman take better care of herself and her house? But after having served her and talked with her, I was instead impressed with her ability to just keep going considering her difficult situation.

In each of these seemingly insignificant stories, the important lesson, that every life is precious, was learned through my trying to serve someone. Have you recently had the opportunity to serve someone in some small way? How have you felt about that person? How have you felt about yourself? When you were engaged in these acts of truly selfless service, how competitive were you feeling? How prideful and arrogant were you feeling? I'd be willing to bet (if I were a betting man), that those acts of true service had a small and subtle, yet potentially powerful impact on how you perceived everything around you.

Assignment:

- Write about your most recent act of selfless service. How did you feel about yourself and those around you while you were serving? (By the way, there is no right or wrong answer.)

CHAPTER SEVEN

SERVING IN SMALL, SIMPLE, AND CONTINUOUS WAYS

"There are no such things as little things." —Stephen R. Covey

Now if you already feel overstressed and overanxious, don't you worry. I assure you that your service does not need to be big or amazing or life-changing. You do not need to mow every lawn in the neighborhood all in one day or babysit all the 2-year-olds in town for free. In fact, I'd recommend that you don't focus on really big service projects at all. If you do that, you'll probably become overwhelmed and you might end up not even taking the first step. Instead, focus on helping in small ways, but try to be consistent. A wise man, who lived hundreds of years ago, wisely observed, "By small and simple things are great things brought to pass."[16]

I love this short account from a man named Dieter F. Uchtdorf. "I once owned a pen that I loved to use during my career as an airline captain. By simply turning the shaft, I could choose one of four colors. The pen did not complain when I wanted to use red ink instead of blue. It did not say to me, "I would rather not write after 10:00 p.m., in heavy fog, or at high altitudes." The pen did not say, "Use me only for important documents, not for the daily mundane tasks." With greatest reliability it performed every task I needed, no matter how important or insignificant. It was always ready to serve."[17]

Serving daily, or weekly, even in small ways, will work wonders in helping you discover your individual worth. The story about my conversation with the lady on the tram in Switzerland and the story about the lady at my work were simple acts which had a life-changing effect on my perception of human value.

I'm sure if you took a minute or two, you could think of many examples where small, simple improvements led to great things. Think of a little child learning to walk or to talk. Children don't suddenly start speaking in whole sentences (at least not the ones I've met). Rather, their progress is made slowly, over time, by making small, simple improvements. First, they are just making sounds, then they say one word or two, then they form a sentence. Before you know it, they are carrying on a full conversation with you and rarely stop talking.

As we get older, it's kind of fascinating how quickly we forget that nearly every worthwhile accomplishment requires small steps over an extended period of time. Again, think of talking, or walking, or reading, or writing, or playing a sport or a musical instrument. These things, and many, many others, are all accomplished through small and simple acts, repeated over, and over, and over. The exact same principle applies when working to discover our self-worth through service. Small, simple acts of service repeated over time will help you in great ways.

Warning Number One Regarding Service: Don't Look Too Far Away

Now remember, as you begin to consider whom you might

serve, don't feel like you have to look too far away. Serving those who are closest to you: your family, your neighbors, your classmates, your friends, and anyone else that might happen to come across your path (even the person who is highest on your "I Hate Forever" list) will be just as effective as serving someone in some foreign country. Just go out and start helping people.

Bonnie L. Oscarson, a religious leader heavily involved in worldwide humanitarian service, once said, "Some of the most significant needs we can meet are within our own families, among our friends... and in our communities. We are touched when we see the suffering and great needs of those halfway around the world, but we may fail to see there is a person who needs our friendship sitting right next to us in class."[18] I find this to be such a wise statement. Remember, try not to get caught up in thinking of some amazing service project that you could do. Just take time to look around you and find people who might need you.

Here is another illustration of this idea: Linda K. Burton, another woman heavily involved in humanitarian service, told the story of a religious leader who, working with others, collected quilts for people in need during the 1990s. "She and her daughter drove a truck filled with those quilts from London to Kosovo. On her journey home she received an unmistakable spiritual impression that sank deep into her heart. The impression was this: 'What you have done is a very good thing. Now go home, walk across the street, and serve your neighbor!'"[19]

I love reading books by the author, Charles Dickens. His books are pretty long and sometimes can get quite complex, but in his stories, he has some great commentary and observations about the society he lived in. In one of his books, *Bleak House*, he has a character, Mrs. Jeleby, who is fanatical about helping people in Africa, yet in her own home, her family, including her poor husband, are totally overlooked and abandoned. The house is chaotic, the children despise their mother, and the mother is totally clueless about it.

Try not to become so focused on the big, easily noticed service projects, that you miss the opportunities "right in [your] way."

Warning Number Two: Don't Procrastinate

Thomas S. Monson once said, "How often have you *intended* to be the one to help? And yet how often has day-to-day living interfered and you've left it for others to help, feeling that 'oh, surely someone will take care of that need…'"[20] Once you've committed yourself to service, beware also of the temptation to put off your service until you have more energy or aren't as stressed or don't have as much homework. If you are anything like me, this temptation will almost certainly come. But an important lesson I've learned (through sometimes painful experience) is that tomorrow usually isn't any less busy or less stressful than today.

The lyrics from the song "Have I Done Any Good in the World Today" serve as a good reminder not to put off until tomorrow what we can and should do today. Here are some of the lines from that song:

> "Have I done any good in the world today? Have I helped anyone in need? Have I cheered up the sad and

made someone feel glad?

Has anyone's burden been lighter today because I was willing to share? Have the sick and the weary been helped on their way, when they needed my help was I there?

"There are chances for work all around just now, opportunities right in our way. Do not let them pass by, saying 'Sometime I'll try', *but go and do something today*."[21]

This is an important reminder to do something today.

Warning Number Three: Don't Lose Patience— Small, Simple, and Consistent

As you begin looking for, and participating in, small, but important acts of service, it is possible that at first you might not notice anything different about yourself. If this happens, please don't worry too much. It would be a mistake to expect the discovering of your worth to occur quickly and all at once. If you are struggling to understand your value, you probably won't suddenly be on top of the world after a couple of acts of service.

Actually, that exact expectation of a quick fix is another reason why I would like to caution against doing some extravagant service project; one probably won't be very effective. But, as the seemingly small acts of service start to add up, your perspective and your understanding will begin to change. You will have taken a very important first step, and perhaps slowly, but surely, you will start to see those around you (including yourself) in a different light. Small and simple *and consistent*, I believe that is the recipe for discovery and change.

Assignment:

- Write down two things you could do to start serving *today*.

CHAPTER EIGHT

A SIMPLE SERVICE ACT— KINDNESS

"Man's greatest happiness comes from losing himself for the good of others."—David O. McKay

Developing the Habit of Kindness

I love poetry. Here is one of my favorite poems (if you hate poetry, don't worry, this one is short).

I have wept in the night

For the shortness of sight

That to somebody's need made me blind;

But I never have yet

Felt a tinge of regret

For being a little too kind.[22]

One of the simplest ways to serve will be to develop the habit of treating others with kindness. In the Merriam-Webster Online Dictionary, one of the definitions it gives for kindness is "of a... helpful nature."[23] I think that's a perfect description: true kindness is helping others, usually in small ways. That kindness, that help, might be in form of a smile, a nice word, a gift, or a hundred other small, simple acts.

And try not to settle for the occasional moments of kindness. Rather, put some effort into developing a habit of kindness. I'm sure you have developed lots of habits during your life, some good, some less good. (Personally, I have a terrible habit of misplacing things. I'm always looking for my glasses, or my wallet, or my keys, or my shoes. It's actually quite maddening). So, why not make the act of being kind, of helping others, a habit. It's probably just about the best habit a person could develop.

Selfish Kindness

But beware of what I call selfish kindness, which is not really kindness at all, rather selfishness masquerading as kindness. This is when we do some "great thing" just so other people can see how wonderful we are. From my experience, it can be really easy to fall into this trap. "Look at me," we are sometimes tempted to say, "I'm the kindest, most wonderful person in the world."

At the school where I teach, there are sometimes students who make a big deal out of helping someone who is really struggling or has special needs. When I was coaching soccer, an autistic boy would often walk past our practice and the players on the team were always so "kind" to him. Don't get me wrong, some of my players were genuinely concerned about that boy and truly wanted to be helpful. However, for some of the players, their "kindness" was just so others could see how "thoughtful" they were. Some of these same soccer players were incredibly unkind to other students at the school, endlessly critiquing and gossiping about others who they thought were not as cool. True kindness often didn't reflect in their day-to-day activities, unless someone was watching.

With respect to discovering your individual worth, this

type of kindness, this fake service, is not helpful at all because when you do these types of things, you're actually just focused on yourself. Remember the principle: *at no point will you understand your worth less than when you are focused on yourself.*

Let me give you another example of this. In my job, one of my colleagues is constantly seeking approval from other people. In order to get this, he is more than willing to do some great acts of generosity. He will drive hours to go visit someone or give lots of money to someone in need. And then, he will tell you about it. (I bet you know people like this, too, right?) However, on a daily basis, he is very rarely truly kind or considerate.

Sadly, the praise this man gets from those around him and the praise my soccer players received for doing very public acts did not actually help them discover their value. In fact, ironically, it did the exact opposite. The attention they received and will continue to receive will not, and cannot, satisfy them. They do things because they want to be appreciated, yet, on the regular, they don't feel appreciated. In fact, most of the time they feel just the opposite: underappreciated. Their view will always be distorted. As we discussed in an earlier chapter, their house will always be built on sand.

Perhaps you feel like I am being a little too harsh in those previous paragraphs and certainly I don't expect anyone to be altruistic all the time. Anybody who knows me well has hundreds of stories they could tell which would prove that I am certainly not perfect. There are many times in my life when I've been a jerk or been unkind or done things just because I wanted attention. Please don't think I'm telling you to be perfect, or that I'm somehow better than these people. I am not. What I am trying to tell you is that kindness, which is a powerful service tool, will only help you discover your worth if you are doing these things *without* the desire for attention or recognition.

Patiently Listen

A simple act of kindness you could begin to implement starting today is being more willing to listen to others. There are lots of people who need someone to talk to but they just don't know whom they can count on to really listen (maybe you are one of these people). They are worried that, when they begin speaking, the other person will judge them or interrupt them or quickly lose interest. And, can you blame them? Let's be honest, a lot of us are not very good listeners. We might pretend to listen or listen with the intent to advise. Only a few people I've met are good at listening in order to understand and empathize.[24]

Because there is such a lack of good listeners in the world, listening would be a perfect place to start your service. Just try to remember that, as Stephen R. Covey says in his fantastic book *Seven Habits of Highly Effective People*, the purpose of your listening should be to "genuinely seek to understand the individual."[25]

Personally, I'm a pretty terrible listener. Sometimes I will listen to someone talk and then, after about 17.35 seconds, my mind starts to wander. (If you don't believe me, ask my wife, she will be more than willing to confirm my claim). However, I do have one or two success stories. Here's one.

Once upon a time, when I was a struggling and starving college student, I worked at a grocery store. It was great. I generally don't like being around people, but for some reason I really enjoyed talking to the customers as they came through my checkout line at the grocery store. One night, as we were nearing closing time, I was talking to one of my fellow employees and I could tell something was wrong. She just wasn't her normal, chatty self. Wanting to be helpful, I asked, "What's wrong?" Her answer: "Nothing."

Of course, I knew she wasn't being totally honest with me, but I didn't want to push it, so I just kept working and making small talk. Then, after about ten minutes of shooting the breeze, she finally opened up. She talked about some of the things she was struggling with and we probably talked for a half hour or more about what was troubling her.

What I learned that day (and what I have had to relearn many, many times since) is that quality listening takes time and patience. Many people have concerns they would like to talk about, stuff that is weighing on their minds, but they aren't going to tell you the innermost secrets of their soul unless they know you are willing to listen and aren't in a rush to do something else or go somewhere else or overwhelm them with your advice or check your phone for anything else that might be more interesting.

As Russell M. Nelson, a renowned heart surgeon and religious leader said, "Everyone has pain somewhere and our challenge is to find out where the pain is. Usually it is not physical pain, but comes in the stress of living... When you meet someone, find out how [you] can help them."[26]

Henry B. Eyring, another religious leader, expressed a similar thought when he said, "When you meet someone, treat them as if they were in serious trouble, and you will be right more than half the time."[27]

Being kind by patiently listening is just one of the simple steps you could take to help you discover your infinite, individual worth and, just as importantly, the worth of the people all around you. Remember, "There are chances for [service] all around just now, opportunities right in our way. Do not let them pass by."

Final Service Thought:

A couple of years ago, I had a student in my class who really struggled to understand her worth. To other students at the school, this would have probably come as a surprise because in so many ways, this girl had so much going for her. She was talented and earned great grades; she was attractive and very outgoing. Despite this, she struggled… a lot. In her mind, her worth was based on her relationship with other people at the school. If her relationships went well, then she was great. But if they went badly, she would start to believe that the world was collapsing around her.

Although she didn't know it, she had absolutely no clue what her true value was. She was looking in the wrong places and taking the wrong steps. What she perceived as her worth actually had nothing to do with her worth. The curse of comparison was very real for her, and, as I mentioned, she had some very challenging days, months, and years.

Fortunately, the summer between her junior and senior

years she had the opportunity to get involved in regular, simple service opportunities. These weren't "change the world" service projects, just simple, organized projects meant to help the people who lived in and around her community. After a couple of months, a truly amazing thing happened to her: she finally began to understand her true worth. I noticed this when she, now a senior, came into my classroom to talk to me. She was talking about her service experiences and she expressed her amazement at how good it felt to serve. But it wasn't just her words that impressed me; her whole countenance had changed. She was positive, happy. Don't get me wrong, she wasn't (and probably still isn't) perfect—remember that this voyage of discovery is a process not an event—but she had certainly gained a deeper understanding of her worth. And that discovery had changed her.

Assignment:

- Get a small notebook and write down all the kindnesses you completed for a week. Write about what you did and how it makes you feel. Try to focus on the small and simple acts.

CHAPTER NINE

STEP TWO TO DISCOVERY— CHOOSE A CHALLENGE

"Success is not final; failure is not fatal. It is the courage to continue that counts." —Winston Churchill

Have you ever tried doing something totally new to you? You saw an activity or a sport, and you thought, "Hey, I want to try that out, even though I have absolutely no idea how"? The next important step in discovering your individual worth, in addition to small acts of service, is choosing to challenge yourself. I would like to encourage you to choose to embrace the challenge of doing something new and difficult. Try some activity you've never done before or begin the process of learning a totally new skill. As you choose a challenge, and experience both success and failure, you will discover so much about yourself. You will begin to see that you possess a certain depth you might not have previously known about.

The spring of 2021 was the first time in the history of Payson High School (that is the school where I teach) where we had a boys and girls lacrosse team. I am lucky enough to be one of the coaches for the girl's lacrosse team and I'll tell you that I have been totally amazed at the number of girls who were willing to come and try a brand-new sport. Of all the girls we had at tryout, not one of them had ever played in an organized lacrosse game (lacrosse is not a very well-known sport in my part of the world). Yet they were willing to give it a try. It was a wonderful learning experience for all of us involved and a powerful reminder for me that a great way to discover your infinite, individual worth is to choose a new challenge.

Here is a short list of potential challenges you might want to try out (I'm sure you will be able to think of a lot more):

- Learn/develop a new skill in the fine arts (music, dancing, art)
- Improve your physical fitness
- Do some sort of challenging physical adventure
- Increase your studying/reading
- Learn a foreign language
- Improve in some social aspect of your life (I hate anything "social," so this would be a huge challenge for me)

Now I know that for some of you, upon reading the first few paragraphs of this chapter, your anxiety might have just gone through the roof. Maybe you hate doing hard things and/or maybe you hate to fail. I know that feeling; I've felt it many times and know that it is not a great feeling to have. Or perhaps your thoughts are on a different level. Maybe you're just thinking, "This is dumb. I don't want to do this. It can't possibly help."

Whatever you might be thinking in this moment, I can only promise you that choosing to challenge yourself will be worth it. Remember the fictional account of my son losing his $100 bill. As he searches high and low and tears his room apart looking for that money, he is very likely to have some very frustrating moments and he might get really discouraged. But as he searches, he learns, and how great will be the reward when he finally makes that discovery. I believe the same thing will happen with you.

Don't Fear or Avoid Failure

In the classes I teach, I have a fair number of students who are totally paralyzed by the fear of failure. They simply cannot handle the thought of performing poorly. Their stress levels concerning their grades sometimes get to be nearly debilitating (Which can be slightly counterproductive since debilitation means they wouldn't be able to do any of their schoolwork or even attend school in the first place). Please, as part of this process, do not worry if you fail occasionally, or a lot. In fact, do not fear failure at all, accept it, embrace it. It will be okay if things don't work out exactly as you want.

Several years ago, my daughter was learning to ride her sweet hand-me-down Buzz Light year bike. At some point in her training, she fell, and I ran over to help her get back up. She was really upset. She wasn't hurt, but she was so frustrated with her lack of bike-riding skill that she looked at me and through tears asked if she could be done riding her bike. Well, if she would have asked to be done because she hated physical exercise and hated bikes, I might have given in, but she had chosen to ride her bike and was having a great time; she was just tired of failing. So, in my most loving tone, I told her "no" she could not stop riding her bike. She needed to get back on the bike and try again. I didn't want her to stop just because it was hard. (Thankfully, she did eventually learn how to ride a bike and is now a master bike rider)

Historical Role Models

Something that helps me personally, as I confront my own fears of failure, is to remember that so many of the great stories from history are about people who also had to confront that same fear. I think of such important historical figures as Winston Churchill, Thomas Edison, and the Wright Brothers; each of whom overcame numerous missteps and mistakes. Both Roosevelt presidents also come to mind in their perseverance in overcoming severe physical handicaps.

And, of course, any such list would be incomplete without mentioning Helen Keller and her teacher Anne Sullivan, who, against all odds, accomplished what some (including me) might consider miraculous. To my thinking, as far as choosing to accept a challenge, Anne Sullivan is an awesome example. Nearly everyone knows the remarkable accomplishments of Helen Keller, but less well-known are those of her truly remarkable teacher Ms. Sullivan, who also led a heroic life in her own right.

Anne Sullivan

Anne's life started with numerous challenges. Her mother died when she was about eight, and her father abandoned her soon after. As a result, at that young age she was sent, along with her brother, to live as orphans in a poor house. A couple of months after this, her brother also tragically died. In addition to these trials, earlier in her life (at age five) she had already been diagnosed with a disease in her eyes. This disease would follow Anne throughout her life and cause severe vision challenges.

In the face of these challenges, Anne had a decision to make. She could choose to drift in homelessness from poor house to poor house or she could choose to challenge herself. Luckily for her, for Helen Keller, and for any student of history, instead of remaining in the poor house, she somehow found the courage to challenge herself, and gained acceptance at a respectable school, the Perkins School. At this school, she continued to challenge herself. It wasn't enough for her to simply be at the Perkins School, she also wanted to excel. Of course, this was not easy. In the beginning, she had basically no reading or writing skills and was often made fun of and critiqued. This was a difficult time for Anne and very humiliating, but she was determined and intent on persevering.

Here was this 14-year-old orphan girl with no previous education who went to this school filled with more educated children from wealthy families, yet she simply wouldn't give up. She was remarkable. By the end of her school experience, she was chosen to give the valedictory address (this honor is given to someone who is at the very top of the class). It was only a year after this that she was asked to be a private tutor for Helen Keller.[28]

Regarding her own experience, Ms. Sullivan, this amazing human being, said the following, "Keep on beginning and failing. Each time you fail, start all over again, and you will grow stronger until you have accomplished a purpose— not one you began with perhaps, but one you'll be glad to remember."[29]

Alexander Graham Bell

Without being too much of a history nerd, can I just give you one more example from history regarding someone who chose to embrace a challenge and who overcame numerous failures: Alexander Graham Bell. He spent his life taking on new challenges and luckily for him, and for us, some of these challenges ended up with tremendous results. As you might know, he invented the telephone, and think how boring life would be without telephones.

But not all the challenges he chose ended up being successful. Sometimes he just straight up failed. On September 19, 1881, United States President James Garfield was shot as he boarded a train in Washington D.C. Surprisingly, the bullet actually remained in his body and he didn't die immediately. There was a belief by some of the doctors that if the bullet was removed, President Garfield's life might be saved, and Bell accepted the challenge of finding a way of removing that bullet. He worked to create a machine that could discover where metal was inside someone's body. Unfortunately (especially for President Garfield), his machine failed to accomplish the task.

Yet even after this well-publicized failure, Mr. Bell would continue to live his life accepting the next challenge that would come his way. He never let failure stop him; it just came with the territory of choosing to challenge himself. In his office hung the words, "Keep Fighting."[30]

Alexander Graham Bell, this great inventor, once said, "Don't keep forever on the public road, going only where others have gone, and following one after the other like a flock of sheep… Leave the beaten track occasionally and dive in the woods. Every time you do so you will be certain to find something that you have never seen before."[31]

Certainly, one of the things you will find, among the many, is your individual worth.

Everyday Role Models

Now, maybe you don't feel like you're on the same level as these more famous figures. You might be thinking, "Well, there is a reason they are so well-known, they are exceptional. I'm just average. I can't do that kind of stuff." If that's the case, let me tell you two other stories, one from the life of one of my students and one from my own life.

As a teacher, one of my absolute favorite things is going to graduation each year. Sitting on the stand and seeing my former students receive their diplomas is a really rewarding experience for me. At one graduation several years ago, a student, who had once survived my history class, gave a fantastic speech about this exact topic of challenging herself. In her speech, she described one of her really challenging high school experiences: she had run for student council and lost. Now to some people, this might not seem like a big deal, but for her, initially, this failure had been really devastating (as it is for many other high schoolers who experience something similar).

Thankfully, she used that failure as a catalyst, instead of as an excuse. She had tried something difficult, had failed, but had then used that failure as motivation to do even more difficult things. In the process she achieved a lot more than the average high schooler. Even more importantly, she discovered vital elements of her individual worth. I'm a pretty forgetful person, but I don't think I will ever forget the power of that speech.

Dance Classes

In my freshmen year at college, I decided to take a dance class. There was just one problem, I was a terrible dancer. Terrible. I had no rhythm (still don't), and my body was incredibly stiff (which apparently isn't a good thing if you want to be a dancer). I was so bad that one of my teachers, my tap dance instructor, once pulled me aside and told me that it looked like I was dancing underwater, due to the fact that I was so far off the beat (in her defense, she tried to be very kind in breaking the news to me). In a different class, intermediate clogging, I got so frustrated with my inability to learn the steps that I walked out into the hall, picked up the nearest object, which happened to be my shoe, and threw it at the wall as hard as I could (good thing I went into the hall, since the walls in the classroom/studio were all glass).

But this total lack of dancing talent didn't deter me. I loved my dance classes and despite my total lack of ability, I took literally dozens of these classes throughout my college experience. The classes weren't easy, and I was frustrated by my terribleness, but I discovered so much about myself that I would never have otherwise discovered. I was discovering, in a very real way, my worth as an individual.

What is Your Challenge?

So, I would like to again encourage you to find something challenging, something difficult that you might possibly enjoy, and give it a try. Stick with it, even if it's hard. Fail, get up, fail again, get up and keep going. If you stick to it, and don't give up, you will discover your individual worth in ways you never could have imagined. The elements of you which you discover in this process were always there, they just needed to be found. And, as an added bonus, you will also learn the very important principle that failure, indeed, is not fatal.

Assignment:

- Find something enjoyable and challenging and try it. Write about your successes and failures. Write about what you have learned about yourself.

CHAPTER TEN

STEP THREE TO DISCOVERY— GIVE GRATITUDE

"If you concentrate on what you don't have, you will never, ever have enough."—Oprah Winfrey

Have you ever heard the hymn, "Count Your Many Blessings"? It begins with the words, "When upon life's billows you are tempest tossed. When you are discouraged, thinking all is lost. Count your many blessings name them one by one..."[32]

Perhaps you've wondered, as I sometimes have, why it is so important to count your blessings when you are discouraged. Of all things, why would that help? Well, I for sure don't know all the reasons, but one thing I have learned is that it is much easier to overcome the curse of comparison if you try to focus on all the good things you have in life instead of focusing on the negative. As two authors put it, "Once you start to recognize the contributions that other people have made to your life— once you realize that other people have seen the value in you—it will transform the way you see yourself. It's this sense of self-worth that opens the door to transforming the world around you."[33]

So, as you begin the process of discovering your individual worth by first, doing small acts of service and second, choosing to challenge yourself, you will then be ready to take the next important step: giving gratitude.

I love this poem about gratitude:

Some murmur when the sky is clear

And wholly bright to view,

If one small speck of dark appear

In their great heaven of blue:

And some with thankful love are filled,

If but one streak of light,

One ray of God's good mercy, gild

The darkness of their night.[34]

George Bailey

It's a Wonderful Life is another movie you absolutely need to watch at some point in your life (preferably sooner rather than later). At one point in the movie the main character, George Bailey, experiences a bit of money trouble (he loses $8,000 which, as you can imagine, would be kind of frustrating). In a moment of self-pity, he exclaims to Clarence, an angel who is sent to help him, "I wish I had never been born." When Clarence hears this, he rightly understands that this as a great opportunity to teach an important lesson and thus grants George his wish.

With the wish granted, the movie then travels back in time and shows how the Bailey family and the town would have been different if George had never existed. Can you guess what George Bailey learns as he witnesses this? He learns that his community, his family, and his friends would *not* be better off if he had never been born. Although he had made mistakes (like losing $8,000), he had also done a lot of good. This realization of his value creates an overpowering sense of gratitude in George's heart and eventually, at the end of the movie, he happily returns to his family (even though he never does find the $8,000).

Although this movie was made back in 1946, the principle we learn from George Bailey, that gratitude and individual worth are closely connected, is still valuable. It is very difficult (if not impossible) to experience one without experiencing the other. In your own journey to discover your individual worth, I'm hoping that you will have a similar experience to that of George Bailey, but in reverse. George discovered his value which caused a deep sense of gratitude. As you look for ways to develop gratitude, I believe you will discover a deeper understanding of your value.

Greener Grass

This is easier said than done though, isn't it? We've all heard the phrase, "The grass is always greener on the other side," and doesn't it seem like sometimes the grass really is a lot greener on the other side? The curse of comparison makes it so hard to be content with what we have and where we are. Maybe you want more friends or different friends. Or you wish you had a car, then you wish had a different car (one that doesn't break down every month, or week). You wish you were in school, then you wish you were out of school.

And of course, social media doesn't help much. When you see the digital lives of the people around you, and when you look at all your own pictures and posts from a happier time, it might seem like it was so much more fun to live in the past, or the future, or somewhere else entirely. I know sometimes I get like this; I get so busy wishing I was somewhere else or wishing I had something else that it becomes really hard for me to be grateful for what I do have.

Several years ago, I taught and coached a girl at the high school who was very talented. She was on the student council, a member of the varsity soccer team, attractive, and funny. Tons of girls at the school would have loved to be in her shoes, but, unfortunately, she had a hard time seeing this. Instead, she was constantly comparing herself to others. As you can imagine, this constant comparison was totally destructive to her self-image, her self-esteem, and her friendship. She had a difficult time being grateful for all the talents she had because she was too busy wishing she was someone else.

Her story—and the stories of many others just like her—has taught me that a shortage of gratitude can potentially turn into a life-altering problem. It will be a huge challenge to try and discover or remember your individual worth if you have a hard time appreciating where you are and who you are.

Think about the house you live in; if you're always noticing all the little things you don't like about your house and always wishing things were different, you'll never learn to appreciate all the good things your house possesses. Your mind will constantly revert to all the worst parts of your current house. When you think, "Gosh, I wish my house was bigger," all you're really thinking is, "This house sure is small."

So it is with life. If you're always saying to yourself, "Golly,

I wish I were somewhere else, doing something else," all you're really saying is, "I don't like where I'm at. I don't see the value of me in the place I'm in right now." If you're wishing for a different life, it will be really hard to see the blessings of your current life, and if you can't see those blessings, you probably won't be able to see your value.

Learn to Look—Appreciate the Present

How can you begin the process of developing a thankful heart? How can you learn to be "more content with the things allotted unto [you]?"[35] Lloyd Newell, a public speaker, and university professor, wrote the following, which has been helpful to me:

"Why is it that life is so hard for some and so much easier for others? Some people seem to have more happiness and opportunities, and others much less. Indeed, life can seem neither fair nor equal."

"There may not be a single formula or step-by-step recipe for peace and happiness in this life. But there are noticeable patterns that can teach us how to cope with life's difficulties and challenges."

"We see such patterns of strength all around us that we can look up to; the mother who suddenly finds herself single does her best to go forward, even though her life has been turned upside down; the dad who has lost his job but somehow stays positive and strong even in the face of rejections and setbacks; the young adult who tries to stay kind and soft-hearted in an often harsh and hardened world; the accident victim who knows that his life will never be like it used to be but does his best to adjust to the new normal."

"What is the consistent pattern in people like these? They certainly weren't blessed with a life of ease or a smooth path. But they all hold on to the hope that things will work out and someday get better. **Instead of counting their grievances or asking, 'Why me?' they remember their blessings. Instead of focusing their thoughts and conversations on what they don't have, they choose to recognize what they do have.** Rather than being consumed by disadvantages and problems, life's unfairness and unevenness, they look for—and find—the good in their lives."

"It's a simple pattern, really: if we focus on what we have rather than what we don't have, we begin to discover the real richness of life. **Blessings are not discovered by accident; they are revealed to those who seek.** In fact, if you look for patterns of strength and endurance in your own life, you'll begin to find that you are stronger than you may think."[36]

This is a powerful lesson from Dr. Newell. If you want to develop a grateful heart, the first step is to just start looking. And the sooner you start looking, the better. The next step is to then turn that act of looking into a habit of looking. Consciously train yourself to look for the good things in your life.

Of course, this won't be easy. There will be times when the lemonade you made from your lemons might just taste really sour and disgusting. But as you practice, and as you remind yourself to focus on what you do have, you will discover, and more powerfully remember, your individual worth. Learn to look.

Take Control of Your Mind

Let me give you one other tip that might prove helpful if you tend to complain or focus on the negative too much. Neil Hahl, one of my many mentors, once told me that if an unwanted thought pops into your head, simply replace it with a wanted thought. Although it's not easy, it really is a basic process: the next time you start to think about the greener grass on the other side, the next time you are tempted to complain or feel self-pity, replace that thought with something else. And it can really be just about anything, just make sure it is something you love and appreciate. As you notice the negative thought coming in, stop that mental motion, and start thinking about something else you are totally comfortable with and grateful for—sports, dancing, music or whatever (for me, it's sports. I love sports).

People who study habits say that one of the keys to breaking a bad habit is recognizing what prompts the bad habit (the cue) and substituting something else in its place.[37] That is what I would encourage you to do. Learn to recognize when negative thoughts of ingratitude are taking up your precious mental space, then practice making that substitution. Of course, you're not going to be very good at this at first, but don't stress, just practice and be patient with yourself and you'll steadily improve. I promise you will discover many blessings and in finding them, you will better understand what it means to find yourself.

You Have the Choice

Keep in mind that this is a decision only you can make;

73

nobody else can make it for you. Nobody else knows your thoughts. That puts you in a powerful position because, although you can't control a lot of things happening in your life (like your curfew), you can control whether you will be grateful. Viktor Frankl, a Nazi Concentration Camp survivor, wrote the following in his well-known book *Man's Search for Meaning*, "We who lived in concentration camps can remember the men who walked through the huts comforting others, giving away their last piece of bread. They may have been few in number, but they offer sufficient proof that everything can be taken from a man but one thing: the last of… human freedoms—to choose one's attitude in any given set of circumstances, [and] to choose one's own way [of life]."[38]

Choose to be grateful.

Discover the Past

As I have already mentioned, I am a high school history teacher, so, as you can imagine, I think learning about the past is pretty exciting (and yes, by writing that, I understand you might now think I'm crazy). But learning about the past can be more than just exciting; as you discover more about those great persons who did great things, it can also be a useful step in both developing your gratitude and understanding your individual worth.

Now, you might be thinking, "Oh please no, don't talk about history. History is the most boring subject on this planet. I would rather watch Little League baseball" (which, in case you have never watched, is barely tolerable). If you are thinking this, let me assure you that I am not asking you to spend hours and hours learning about your Great-Great-Great-Great Uncle Ferdinand or to read all six volumes of *The Decline and Fall of the Roman Empire*. I just want to encourage you to learn a little bit about those who've gone before you and find out what they did with their lives.

What You Will Discover

As you do just a little bit of historical searching, you will first discover how much your ancestors struggled, and then you will discover how much they were able to accomplish despite (and sometimes because of) their struggles. You will find out that life has many challenges, but you will also learn, just like so many people throughout history have learned, that challenges and struggles do not have to be stumbling blocks. They can just as easily be stepping-stones to an increased understanding of human worth.

Let me give you an example. When my great-grandmother was a little girl, she lived in Denmark. As a young adult, she decided to change her religion. Do you know what happened to her when she made this pivotal decision? She was kicked out of her house and told to never come back. Can you imagine how hard that must have been? Yet, somehow, she found the strength to endure that terrible trial and made her way to the United States and we, her descendants, are nothing but thankful for her tremendous courage. When I acknowledge her remarkable story, it helps me to understand her value and the value of so many others like her who have persevered through trials I can barely understand.

In addition to your own ancestors, other events and people from history can also help you better understand your individual worth. Anybody who does a little historical studying will easily find stories of those whose lives were so difficult, yet who kept going. You might learn about those people living in London in 1940 who basically had to suffer getting their houses bombed every night for months. Or maybe you will learn about those who had to travel the Trail of Tears, who were kicked out of their lands simply because they were a different race. Or perhaps you will read about the millions of people who struggled through the economic challenges of the Great Depression, one of the darkest decades of our nation's history. And these are just a few examples, there are so many more.

Thomas Jefferson

I am sure that, even if you've slept through every history class, you've heard of Thomas Jefferson. And I'm hoping that not only have you heard of him, but that you also know that Jefferson played a vital role in the foundation of the United States. However, even though he was influential in our Founding, Thomas Jefferson is not my favorite person. In fact, there are some things he did during his life that are simply infuriating.

In spite of this, when I recently read a book about his life, I was moved by some of the challenges he faced and felt a deep sense of gratitude for what he endured and accomplished. Near the end of the American Revolution, Jefferson had two events occur in quick succession which might have been insurmountable to other people: his wife died and the capital of Virginia, where he was governor, was taken by the British. Jon Meacham wrote in his book about this moment:

"[Jefferson] was nearly forty years old, and, until recently, had never failed at anything. A favored son, a brilliant student, a legislator of his state at age twenty-five, the author of The Declaration of Independence at thirty-three, and the governor of Virginia at thirty-six. Thomas Jefferson was accustomed to public success and popular praise…

"No more. His beloved wife had died. His administration of Virginia in the face of the attacks of Benedict Arnold and Charles Cornwallis was widely seen as little less than disastrous."[39]

From my perspective, the death of a spouse alone would be hard enough to overcome, but to also basically fail as the governor of your state at the same time would surely be overwhelming to many. But Jefferson fought through these two major setbacks. And, importantly, it was only after these challenges that he became an ambassador to France, Secretary of State to President Washington, Vice President to John Adams, and, finally, our third president. Our nation would have been much different without the persistence of Thomas Jefferson.

Perhaps you have had, up to this point, a very difficult life, a life much harder than anything I've had to experience, and harder even than some of the people I have mentioned (maybe *you* were the one who got kicked out of your house). Nonetheless, I promise you, if you look through history, you will find someone or some event which will help you feel more gratitude. And when they make you feel that, I think you will be pleasantly surprised by the accompanying understanding of your own worth.

77

Assignment:

- Start a gratitude journal. Each day write down two things you are grateful for. See how long you can go without repeating.

CHAPTER ELEVEN

STEP FOUR TO DISCOVERY— DISCOVER DEITY

"The only thing that matters now is everything You think of me. In You I find my worth, in You I find my identity." —Lauren Daigle

The ideas and principles which I have already discussed in this book are very important to me. I have no doubt that they will help you discover your individual worth and escape the curse of comparison. However, this book would be incomplete if I didn't include what I think is the *most* important principle in understanding your individual worth: discovering deity.

To fully understand your infinite, individual worth at its deepest level, I believe it is important to understand two extremely valuable principles, both of which are closely related. They are:

1) There is a God who created you.

and...

2) This God cares specifically about you.

Perhaps you were born into a religious culture, or perhaps you weren't. Maybe, as you've grown up, you've thought about God a lot, or maybe you haven't. Whatever your situation, I want you to stop for a moment and be completely honest with yourself while answering these two questions: 1) Do you believe in God? 2) Do you believe there is a God who cares about you?

Now just to clarify, it's important that you understand that I know a lot of people who have very positive views of themselves but have no religious beliefs at all. Without a belief in God, it is totally possible to understand that you are important and that your life has value. I am definitely not saying you can't understand your individual worth if you don't believe in God. I am not saying that all. What I am saying is that when you know that God, the most wonderful presence in the universe, loves even little old you, then you can come to an even more powerful and deeper appreciation of how much value your life has. It is with this knowledge that you will realize even more profoundly how very precious each life is.

Earlier in this book I compared discovering your individual worth to that of mining for gold. If we compare your individual worth to gold, then discovering deity is like discovering the motherload.

Regarding this principle, I would like to return to a quote I cited in chapter four. As I hope you remember (after all this isn't that long of a book), in that chapter I gave a quote from Max Lucado's *You Are Special* which ended with Eli saying to Punchinello,

> "Who are they to give stars or dots? They're Wemmicks just like you. What they think doesn't matter, Punchinello."

I would now like to continue with that quote. The speaker Eli, who is the creator of the Wemmicks, then continued,

> "What they think doesn't matter, Punchinello. All that matters is what I think. And I think you are pretty

special."

Punchinello laughed.

"Me, special? Why? I can't walk fast. I can't jump. My paint is peeling. Why do I matter to you?"

Eli looked at Punchinello...and spoke very slowly.

"Because you're mine. That's why you matter to me.'"

The belief that you matter to God, to your Creator, no matter what personality traits you have, can be powerful. Yes, you can definitely know you have individual worth without understanding this powerful principle, but there is something wonderful about discovering His loving kindness for you; discovering that you really are an important person in God's eyes.

Alma the Younger

In the collection of ancient writings which I mentioned in chapter four, there is a story about a man named Alma the Younger." When he was young, this man, Alma, thought God and religion were a total waste of time. In fact, he made it his goal in life to persecute as many believers as he could and tried his absolute best to ruin the church his family belonged to. Then, one day, as he was going around being a jerk, he had his own personal, religious experience. He had a life-changing vision and came to know personally that God existed and knew who he was.

After Alma had this epiphany, he began to understand that even though he was doing terrible things, God still loved him. This realization totally changed the trajectory of Alma's life. He began to view himself and others in a

81

completely different light and began to understand that he, his family, and even his worst enemies, had value. As he said later in his life regarding those enemies, "their souls are precious."[40] He knew that if God still loved him, even after all his mistakes, then God certainly loved everyone else as well.

Where to Start

Perhaps, as I gave this quote from *You are Special* and told this story about Alma the Younger, you are wondering where to even begin this process of discovering deity. If you are thinking this, no worries, it is a very valid concern and one that has occupied the thoughts of many people (some of whom were really smart) throughout the centuries. You are in some pretty good company.

A good starting point is remembering that you shouldn't feel like you have to do some big thing or have some earth-shattering experience. What I said about service also applies to discovering deity, "By small and simple things are great things brought to pass."

Keeping that in mind, here are some possible ideas of where to begin.

Nature

As I am writing this, I am sitting out in my backyard, under the trees, listening to the birds constant chirping (I live in a small town, so some days birds are the loudest thing I hear). Sitting here, it strikes me that being out in nature is a wonderful place to think deeper about life and life's purpose. This type of peaceful, outdoor environment can be a great place to draw closer to God, to understand the divine a little better. Throughout religious history, many of the great ones have had powerful spiritual experiences while out in nature. Think of Moses and the Ten Commandments or Peter, James, and John on the Mount of Transfiguration.

In fact, Jesus himself often spent solitary moments in nature in order to connect with God. In Mark 1:35 it says, "And in the morning, rising up a great while before day, [Jesus] went out, and departed into a solitary place, and there prayed." In our world with so much noise and bustle, a solitary place might sometimes seem hard to find. Nature can be that place (just make sure the birds aren't too loud).

Sacred Music

But being out in nature certainly isn't your only option. From ninth grade until after I graduated from high school, I was member of a children's choir directed by Beverly Thomas called the Utah Valley Concert Choir. During the school year we met every Saturday morning from 7:00 a.m. to 9:00 a.m. and then each summer we went on a tour. (We were able to tour such scenic places as the United Kingdom, Washington D.C., and the great state of Wyoming.) In our touring, practicing, and performing, we sang almost exclusively religious songs. Looking back on my high school life, I don't think it would be an exaggeration to say that nearly every time I felt God's presence as a teenager occurred while I was singing with that choir or listening to other religious music. And I know I wasn't the only one who had these types of experiences. There were other choir members who similarly had powerful spiritual experiences resulting from beautiful, sacred music.

Scripture

Another possible option for discovering deity is to read great religious literature. Now I know the thought of reading religious literature can sometimes be daunting because some of these writings, books like the Old Testament and New Testament, are often written in pretty complicated language (more complex than what you might read on your social media feed at least). But if you give it a try, you might be pleasantly surprised with what you discover and experience. And remember, as far as scripture is concerned, a little goes a long way. Five to ten minutes a day is more than enough to begin your process of discovery. As one religious leader promised, "As you read [the scriptures], your minds will be enlightened, and your spirits will be lifted. At first it may seem tedious, but that will change into a wondrous experience with thoughts and words of things divine"[41]

When I think of my own spiritual experiences, one that often comes to mind occurred as I was walking back to my dorm my freshman year of college. When I moved away from home that first year of college, for the first time in my life, I regularly read and studied the scriptures. I don't remember all the details of the experience, but it was the middle of the semester and I had just survived a long, stressful day of school (I think just about every day of my freshmen year of college was stressful). It was late at night and I was walking across campus past a building called the Jesse Knight Building. As I was walking, out of the blue I had the most peaceful feeling wash over me. Actually, I still remember that feeling today it was so overwhelming. As I was trying to understand this sudden feeling that had come, I had the distinct impression come into my heart that God was pleased with my reading the scriptures. Not that I was perfect or anything like that; simply that God approved of the direction of my life. It was a remarkable and life-altering event for me. Very powerful.

Prayer

Of course, it would be a mistake to overlook the power of prayer. As one hymn says, "Prayer is the soul's sincere desire."[42] Similar to reading the scriptures, the act of praying can also sometimes seem daunting. You might be thinking to yourself, "How am I honestly supposed to go about communicating with a God?" And, perhaps even more overwhelming, you might have no idea what to expect regarding possible answers. To add to those concerns, many religions have totally different ways of praying. All of these issues can definitely lead to some hesitancy.

If you have any of these feelings and are not sure how to begin praying, I would simply advise you to speak to God as if you were talking to someone you love and respect and who cares a lot about you and your wants and your needs. You don't need to use flowery language or complicated words (as the New Testament says, "Avoid vain repetitions"[43]). You just simply need to talk. Say the words out loud or in your head, it doesn't matter. God will hear them either way.

Religious Gatherings

And finally, depending on your situation, a wonderful way to discover deity might be to attend a religious service.

When you think about it, religious services often combine many of the elements I have already listed: peaceful environment, sacred music, religious literature, and prayer. Now I have to admit that for me personally as a teenager, the thought of attending a religious service where I had never been and where I didn't know anybody would have scared me to death, but if you feel like that would be a great place for you to start, go for it.

Four Keys

Although your method of discovering deity will likely be different from mine, and the way in which God responds to you will also probably differ, there are still four general points that I think would be helpful to remember in your search.

The first point is to reassure you that, no matter your current belief level, if you seek God, you will find God. As Jesus says in the Book of Matthew, "Ask, and it shall be given you; seek, and ye shall find; knock, and it shall be opened unto you: For every one that asketh receiveth; and he that seeketh findeth; and to him that knocketh it shall be opened."[44] I totally believe this, so don't be afraid and give it a try.

The second point is the reminder that in your search for deity, it is often helpful to look for God in the peaceful places. As it says in the book of 2 Kings (a book in the Old Testament) "The Lord was not in the wind; and after the wind an earthquake, but the Lord was not in the earthquake. After the earthquake a fire; but the Lord was not in the fire; and after the fire a still small voice."[45] I don't know about you, but "still" and "small" sound peaceful. So, search in peaceful spots where you will be able to hear a still, small voice (wherever those spots might be). I like this thought from Natalie Brenner: "I began realizing… it was possible to find [God] in the immense stillness, the hidden parts of my heart. He was always there in my hiddenness."[46]

The third point is to not let your expectations get in the way of your experience and don't try to force a spiritual experience.[47] A lot of times, when thinking about individual religious experience, we might be drawn to the exceptional experiences—the stories of people who have seen spiritual beings or had overwhelming enlightening visions. But if we are trying to force ourselves to have such an experience, or only expect to have such an experience, then we will likely miss out on powerful, yet individualized answers. Remember, exceptional experiences are just that, the exception. As the character John Newton observes in the movie *Amazing Grace*: "God sometimes does his work with gentle drizzle, not great storms."

The fourth, and final point, which goes along with the third, is to be patient. Your spiritual experience might come right off the bat and it might come in a quick and easily recognizable way. But it might not. For whatever reason, it might *not* come in a quick or easily recognizable manner. You might have to wait a little and struggle a little before you get any sort of answer. For whatever reason, it might not come quickly or easily.

It might also be helpful to remember that discovering deity isn't necessarily just a one-time thing. It is more of a journey than an event. After you have your first spiritual experience, there will come other times when you'll need other answers, and those might require even more patience. Let me tell you two stories which show how this process of finding God can be a journey of a lifetime.

Joseph in Egypt

I've always been fascinated by the story of Joseph in Egypt from the book of Genesis in the Old Testament. When Joseph was young, God told him in a dream that he would someday rule over his brothers. Since Joseph was one of the youngest, I imagine this news might have made him feel pretty good about himself. I know that if one day I was told that I would rule over my six brothers, I would feel pretty awesome.

But, do you know what happens next in the story? After he is told he is going to rule over his brothers, those same brothers take him, throw him into a pit, threaten to kill him, and then sell him into slavery. And as annoying as that might have been for Joseph, his situation then gets only worse (if that was possible). After being forced into slavery, he is then thrown into prison because of a false accusation and is forced to languish there for who knows how long. Can you imagine what he must have been thinking during his darkest hours in that prison cell? First, he is forced to be a slave, now a prison inmate. Talk about the need for patience and waiting on the Lord. I'm sure there were times when he wondered what was going on. If I had been in his shoes, I'm sure there would have been many times when I would have given God a piece of my mind. "What am I doing here?" I would have complained more than once.

Yet, Joseph waits on God, and the reward for his patience

is remarkable. Eventually, he becomes the second in command in Egypt, he returns to his family, and God shows Joseph many miracles. I can't even imagine how Joseph's understanding of his own worth must have developed because of these experiences.

The Currant Bush

Another story I really like was told over fifty years ago by a man named Hugh B. Brown. In this story, he explains an experience where he learns the importance of patience in developing and understanding God's love. (I should give you a little warning: this story is a bit long. But I love it and I think it might be helpful. I know it was very helpful to me when I was a teenager.)

Sixty-odd years ago, I was on a farm in Canada... I went out one morning and found a currant bush that was at least six feet high. I knew that it was going all to wood. There was no sign of blossom or of fruit. So, I got my pruning shears and went to work on that currant bush, and I clipped it and cut it down until there was nothing left but a little clump of stumps.

And as I looked at them, I yielded to an impulse, which I often have, to talk with inanimate things and have them talk to me. It's a ridiculous habit. It's one I can't overcome. As I looked at this little clump of stumps, there seemed to be a tear on each one, and I said, "What's the matter, currant bush? What are you crying about?"

And I thought I heard that currant bush speaks. It seemed to say, "How could you do this to me? I was making such wonderful growth. I was almost as large as the fruit tree and the shade tree, and now you have cut me down… How could you do it? I thought you were the gardener here."

I believed I had heard from the currant bush so much I answered it.

"Look, little currant bush, I am the gardener here, and I know what I want you to be. If I let you go the way you want to go, you will never amount to anything. But someday, when you are laden with fruit, you are going to think back and say, 'Thank you, Mr. Gardener, for cutting me down, for loving me enough to hurt me.'"

Ten years passed, and I found myself in Europe. I had made some progress in the First World War in the Canadian army. In fact, I was a field officer, and there was only one man between me and the rank of general, which I had cherished in my heart for years. Then he became a casualty. And the day after, I received a telegram from London from General Turner, who was in charge of all Canadian officers. The telegram said, "Be in my office tomorrow morning at ten o'clock."

. . .

I went to London. I walked into the office of the general. I saluted him smartly, and he replied to my salute as higher officers usually do to juniors—sort of a "Get out of the way, worm." Then he said, "Sit down, Brown."

I was deflated. I sat down. And he said, "Brown, you are entitled to this promotion, but I cannot make it. You have qualified and passed the regulations, you have had the experience, and you are entitled to it in every way, but I cannot make this appointment."

. . .

Finally, he came back and said, "That's all, Brown." I saluted him, less heartily than before, and went out. On my way back… I thought every turn of the wheels that clacked across the rails was saying, "You're a failure. You must go home and be called a coward by those who do not understand."

And bitterness rose in my heart until I arrived, finally, in my tent, and I rather vigorously threw my cap on the cot… I clenched my fist, and I shook it at heaven, and I said, "How could you do this to me, God? I've done everything that I knew how to do… I was making such wonderful growth, and now you've cut me down. How could you do it?"

And then I heard a voice. It sounded like my own voice, and the voice said, "I am the gardener here. I know what I want you to be. If I let you go the way you want to go, you will never amount to anything. And someday, when you are ripened in life, you are going to shout back across the time and say, 'Thank you, Mr. Gardener, for cutting me down, for loving me enough to hurt me.'"[48]

A Return to Junior High

I started this book by telling you about how much I hated middle school and junior high school. To conclude this chapter, let's return to that period. As I mentioned earlier, that time period was really challenging. I should clarify however that school hadn't always been miserable for me, in fact I had actually really enjoyed elementary school. In elementary school I had had some friends, I had loved recess (who doesn't), and I had done well on my schoolwork and assignments.

But going to middle school presented several challenges. To begin with, our middle school had five elementary schools feed into it, which meant that there were lots and lots of new classmates. As a shy, awkward, little sixth-grader, I had no idea how to handle this change. In addition, many of the kids who had been my friends in elementary school, found other friends. For one reason or another, I no longer fit in their social sphere. As middle school progressed, I did have some friends who were (and still are) great people, but I didn't feel like I had any really close friends; nobody that I could share my deepest, darkest secrets with (and as you know, every teenager needs somebody like that).

And oh, how I hated the noise and the mass of humanity in this new school. As I walked the halls between classes, I felt totally overwhelmed by the pack of the crowds and all the kids talking and laughing. Elementary school had not been like that. In elementary the halls had been much quieter and much calmer. And being in the cafeteria each day for lunch was an almost unbearable sensory experience, with all the hordes of kids and mind-numbing noises. Even today, twenty-five years later, those memories still create some anxiety in me.[49]

Middle school also brought the added element of boyfriends and girlfriends which was a social experience totally beyond my already limited abilities. I literally did not have the ability to carry on a normal conversation with a member of the opposite sex. Granted, a lack of social skills might have been okay if I had been amazingly good-looking or the star of the basketball team, but I wasn't one of those either.

In addition, kids in middle school were much meaner to me than they had been in elementary school. To this day, I'm not exactly sure why kids get meaner as they get older, but they do. I got punched and tripped a lot more. I got made fun of a lot more.

To add to all this, suddenly my good grades in school became a mark against me. In elementary, most kids respected me because I did well on tests and assignments. Now that was no longer the case. Instead of respecting me, this was just one more thing that they could laugh at me for (unless they needed help on an assignment or test, then they were nice for a day or two). All in all, it was pretty painful.

With all of this change, the confidence and self-esteem I had developed in elementary school plummeted and, as you can imagine, I was struggling big time. Now as I told you in the first chapter, this isn't to say that I didn't have any good times. I do have some very positive memories from that time period. I loved my orchestra class and my orchestra teacher Mrs. Dunford (she was the very best) and I did meet some new people who were very kind to me. In addition, Matt Tolman and Alan Johansen did their best to make me feel accepted. But even with those positive experiences, as the sixth grade passed and I entered seventh grade and then eighth grade, I felt like the challenges were going to slowly overwhelm me.

It is perhaps no surprise then that during these years there were many times when I contemplated suicide. There were many days when I simply didn't want to be where I was at and I just didn't know how to get anywhere else. Luckily for me, my suicidal thoughts never did pass the contemplation stage, and I never made an attempt, but even thinking about suicide can be a scary experience.

What Saved Me

As I look back on those days, without a doubt the most important reason I never attempted to take my own life was because I knew there was a God, and I knew God cared about me. I just knew it and that knowledge very literally saved me. Whenever I would seriously consider making an attempt, the thought that would enter my mind and overwhelm all the other darker thoughts was, "God does not want you to end your life. God loves you." I do not think it is an exaggeration to say that belief in deity saved my life many times. This belief provided a powerful protection for me and it is because of this experience that I have no doubt that such a belief can do that for you as well.

Obviously, in your own personal spiritual journey, I can't tell you what will work best for you or what your spiritual experience will be like. Your experiences might be similar to some of mine or they might be of a totally different nature. Whatever happens, I know that if you make the effort, God will speak to you in a way that will make sense to you and will be the most helpful for you to understand.[50] In any case, I can promise you that these experiences when you discover deity, in whatever way they come, will help you understand that God knows you and cares about you, and that you have infinite, individual worth. You will have hit the motherload.

Assignment:

- Find a peaceful place and try to let God communicate His love to you. What did you experience?

CHAPTER TWELVE

CONCLUSION—ESCAPING THE CURSE OF COMPARISON

"'Remember,' Eli said as the Wemmick walked out the door, 'you are special because I made you. And I don't make mistakes.'" —Max Lucado

It Will Be Worth It

Perhaps, you've noticed that this book is relatively short. It is this way for two reasons. 1.) I'm not smart enough to think of much more to say without boring you to death, and 2.) The change that I hope to create doesn't really come through simply reading this book. True change will only come through acting on the principles outlined here. Whereas the book is short, the actual process takes much more time.

However, I can assure you that the process will be worth it, it will work. I can make that promise because I've seen it work in my life and in the life of others. It is possible to resist the curse of comparison and all its challenges. You can do this by developing the ability to see your infinite, individual worth and the worth of the many people around you.

Remember, no matter who you are and what you have done (or haven't done), you have infinite, individual worth and nothing, not anything, can change that.

As you serve in small ways and choose to accept difficult

challenges, as you develop an attitude of gratitude by appreciating the present and learning from the past, and especially as you discover deity, you will discover your true worth and will be able to resist the curse of comparison more effectively.

What will your reward be when you escape from this culture, when your infinite, individual worth becomes the lens through which you see yourself? Your reward will be peace, an amazing, wonderfully peaceful joy. You will be more content with who you are on the inside and what is going on around you on the outside.

There Will Still Be Challenges

However, even with your new understanding of these principles and your newfound ability to resist those ever-present comparisons, life will still be challenging. Hard times will still, unfortunately, regularly find their way into your life. Challenges, stresses, and anxieties might still occasionally overwhelm you. I know that for me, and for basically every other person I know, life still has many challenges. I still have days when I don't want to get out of bed, or days when, at about lunchtime, all I want to do is go back to bed.

And so, with all that is going on around you, even after understanding these principles, you might start to slip back into the habit of comparing yourself to others. You might begin again to wish that you were someone else or somewhere else. It will be easy to fall back into the habit of believing that the value the outside world gives you is your true value; but, when these times come, as they certainly will, just keep pushing through. You will have good days and you will have less-good days; it will be difficult, but you can do it, just keep at it. Don't give up on the process. I believe in you.

Thank you for reading.

ABOUT
KHARIS PUBLISHING

KHARIS PUBLISHING is an independent, traditional publishing house with a core mission to publish impactful books, and channel proceeds into establishing mini-libraries or resource centers for orphanages in developing countries, so these kids will learn to read, dream, and grow. Every time you purchase a book from Kharis Publishing or partner as an author, you are helping give these kids an amazing opportunity to read, dream, and grow. Kharis Publishing is an imprint of Kharis Media LLC. Learn more at
https://www.kharispublishing.com.

Citated Works / Reference

[1] Holland, Jeffrey R., "An High Priest of Good Things to Come", *Ensign*, November 2000.

[2] James 3:10

[3] Kraft, Houston, *Deep Kindness: A Revolutionary Guide for the Way We Think, Talk, and Act in Kindness,* Tiller Press, 2020, p. 109

[4] The story of the wise and foolish men is found in St. Matthew 7:24-27

[5] By the way, my friend Stephen wasn't the only one who had to endure these late-night therapy sessions. Ryan, Lane, Richard, Robb, Kyle and Jeffrey also had their fair share.

[6] These verses can be found in 1 Corinthians 12.

[7] As an example, dictionary.com defines self-worth as "the sense of one's own value or worth as a person; self-esteem; self-respect."

[8] Lucado, Max, *You are Special*, Crossway, 1997, p. 25

[9] Kraft, *Deep Kindness*, p. 110

[10] This collection of writings is called The Book of Mormon.

[11] The Book of Mormon, Ether 6:5-7

[12] Hinckley, Gordon B., "Forget Yourself", BYU Campus Devotional, March 6, 1977

[13] Monson, Thomas S., "Service Brings Joy", *Ensign*

https://www.churchofjesuschrist.org/prophets-and-apostles/unto-all-the-world/service-brings-joy?lang=eng

[14] Christopher Reeve, *Still Me*, Cambria Productions, 1998, p. 5.

[15] The parable of the Good Samaritan is found in St. Luke 10.

[16] The Book of Mormon, Alma 37:6

[17] Elder Dieter F. Uchtdorf, "Pride and the Priesthood", *Ensign*, October 2010.

[18] Bonnie L. Oscarson, "The Needs before Us," *Ensign or Liahona*, October 2017

[19] Linda K. Burton, "I Was a Stranger," *Ensign or Liahona*, May 2016, 15.

[20] Thomas S. Monson, "What Have I Done for Someone Today," *Ensign or Liahona*, November 2009.

[21] Hymn book for the Church of Jesus Christ of Latter-day Saints. Hymn 223

[22] Quoted by Thomas S. Monson in "Never Alone", *Ensign* or *Liahona*, May 1991

[23] Merriam-webster.com

[24] I love this definition of empathy from the Greater Good Magazine: Emotion researchers generally define empathy as the ability to sense other people's emotions, coupled with the ability to imagine what someone else might be thinking or feeling.
https://greatergood.berkeley.edu/topic/empathy/definition

[25] Covey, Stephen R. *The 7 Habits of Highly Effective People: Restoring the Character Ethic*. New York: Free Press, 2004, p. 239

[26] Dew, Sheri *Insights from a Prophet's Life: Russell M. Nelson*, Deseret Book Company, 2019, p. 189

[27] Eyring, Henry B., "Try, Try, Try," *Ensign, November*, 2018

[28] All this information was found on the Perkins School for the Blind website.
Https://www.perkins.org/history/people/anne-sullivan

[29]https://www.brainyquote.com/quotes/anne_sullivan_169987

[30] Bader, Bonnie, *Who was Alexander Graham Bell*, Penguin Workshop, p. 100

[31] Ibid, pp. 99-100

[32] Hymnbook for the Church of Jesus Christ of Latter-day Saints. Hymn 239

[33] Smith, Jeremy Adam, et al, *The Gratitude Project*, New Harbinger Publications Inc., p. 7

[34] Richard Chevenix Trench https://www.bartleby.com/360/4/172.html

[35] Neal A. Maxwell, "Content with the Things Allotted Unto Us." *Ensign* or *Liahona*, May 2000.

[36] Music and the Spoken Word, May 6, 2018, emphasis added.

[37] Two fantastic books on habit forming are *Atomic Habits* by James Clear and *The Power of Habit* by Charles Duhigg

[38] Frankl, Victor, *Man's Search for Meaning*, New York: Simon and Schuster, 1963, p. 104.

[39] Meacham, Jon *Thomas Jefferson: The Art of Power,* Random House: New York, 2012, p. 153

[40] The Book of Mormon, Alma 31:35

[41] Gordon B. Hinckley, "The Light within You," *Ensign*, May 1995, 99.

[42] Hymnbook for the Church of Jesus Christ of Latter-day Saints. Hymn 239

[43] St. Matthew 16:7

[44] St. Matthew 7:7-8

[45] 1 Kings 19:11-16

[46] Natalie Brenner, *This Undeserved Life: Uncovering the Gifts of Grief and The Fullness of Life.* https://www.goodreads.com/quotes/tag/hiddenness

[47] Boyd K. Packer, "Reverence Invites Revelation", *Ensign*, November 1991

[48] https://speeches.byu.edu/talks/hugh-b-brown/god-gardener/

[49] I love the book *Quiet* by Susan Cane. That book has helped me understand that I'm not alone in middle school being a sensory overload experience.

[50] The Book of Mormon, 2 Nephi 31:3

www.ingramcontent.com/pod-product-compliance
Lightning Source LLC
LaVergne TN
LVHW051422080426
835508LV00022B/3198